T0195936

MINDFULNESS
and Sport Psychology
for Athletes:

Awareness Is Your Most Important Mental Tool

Kristine M. Eiring, PhD and
Colleen M. Hathaway, DC

BALBOA.PRESS
A DIVISION OF HAY HOUSE

Balboa Press books may be ordered through booksellers or by contacting:

Balboa Press
A Division of Hay House
1663 Liberty Drive
Bloomington, IN 47403
www.balboapress.com
1 (877) 407-4847

Because of the dynamic nature of the Internet, any web addresses or links contained in this book may have changed since publication and may no longer be valid. The views expressed in this work are solely those of the authors and do not necessarily reflect the views of the publisher, and the publisher hereby disclaims any responsibility for them.

The author of this book does not dispense medical advice or prescribe the use of any technique as a form of treatment for physical, emotional, or medical problems without the advice of a physician, either directly or indirectly. The intent of the author is only to offer information of a general nature to help you in your quest for emotional and spiritual well-being. In the event you use any of the information in this book for yourself, which is your constitutional right, the author and the publisher assume no responsibility for your actions.

Any people depicted in stock imagery provided by Getty Images are models, and such images are being used for illustrative purposes only.
Certain stock imagery © Getty Images.

Print information available on the last page.

ISBN: 978-1-9822-4157-5 (sc)
ISBN: 978-1-9822-4159-9 (hc)
ISBN: 978-1-9822-4158-2 (e)

Library of Congress Control Number: 2020901553

Balboa Press rev. date: 01/17/2020

Mindfulness is an ancient Buddhist practice
which has relevance for our present-day lives.
This relevance has nothing to do with Buddhism
per se or with becoming a Buddhist, but it has
everything to do with waking up and living
in harmony with oneself and with the world.
It has to do with examining who we are, with
questioning our view of the world and our place
in it, and with cultivating some appreciation
for the fullness of each moment we are alive.

Most of all, it has to do with being in touch.

— Jon Kabat Zinn —

This book is dedicated our Fathers

My dad shared his passion of sports and competing with me. He impacted my life more than he will ever know. He was an excellent athlete in his own right, but he also coached. As a young girl, I tagged along with him. I watched him coach youth boys basketball and baseball, adult men's basketball, and eventually my youth girls softball team. I know my dad through sport …and because of sport. It is my language with him. I am grateful to him for sharing his passion of competing with me. He definitely has had a profound impact on my life, my love of competing, and also my profession of helping other athletes. His words of, "Let's play," will always stay with me.

— Kris —

My dad was my first coach and one of the best coaches I had during my athletic career. He was an excellent three-sport athlete and taught me that no one can out work me. He used to say, "They might be bigger or faster than you, but you can work harder than them." Little did I know that my dad was also teaching me about having a mental game. He spoke regularly about having a 'poker face' and an internal drive of extreme intensity. I am grateful to him for his leadership, coaching and constant support.

— Colleen —

CONTENTS

CHAPTER 1

MINDFULNESS: INTRODUCTION

*A*s **Deb** *begins her first pole vault practice approach down the runway, another athlete standing on the side accidentally drops her pole onto the runway, causing Deb to abruptly stop her practice run. She immediately reacts to the disruption with frustration and anger. Quickly, her thoughts turn to how rude and unaware the other athlete was to drop her pole. Deb starts to glare at the other athlete, so she knows how upset she is, but Deb also loses her focus. What will Deb do to regain her focus for competing and come back to the present moment?*

Mindfulness and Mental Tools

This book is for athletes who want to build a strong mental practice as part of their overall training program. Many athletes understand that the mental aspects of training and competing are just as important as the physical aspects. The concepts in this book are designed for all athletes and can be used for building your own individualized mental training program as it relates to your sport.

Athletes of all levels seek tools and information to help build a stronger mental game and to become more emotionally resilient, in order to gain a competitive edge and have peak performance moments. Mindfulness is gaining recognition, through research and practice, as one of the most significant mental tools for athletes.

In this book you will learn:

- The meaning and benefits of mindfulness
- The application of mindfulness, along with other mental tools, within your sport
- Mindfully recovering after practices and performances

Many sport psychology books and workbooks provide a basic outline of various mental skills that athletes can use to help their performance. However, this book is different because it links mental skills with the concept of mindfulness. The basic idea of mindfulness is simple:

You can change habits only through awareness or 'being in touch'.

By following the suggestions in this book, an athlete can learn the process of mindfulness and utilize this to make present-moment mental decisions that assist with focus; or change of focus. The end result of this change is a new thought process associated with enhanced athletic performance. Mindfulness is a powerful vehicle for change because it brings the athlete to the only moment of importance—the present moment.

**"What percent of your game is mental?
The exact amount is unknown.
You make the mental choice every
day to train your body. Make the
same choice to train your brain."**

– Kris Eiring, PhD –

Think about Deb the pole vaulter for a moment:

Ultimately, she performed poorly at this meet and after the meet blamed the other competitor for her performance. In this situation, in the fraction of a second in which Deb made the decision to continue her focus on the other athlete and her rudeness, and something that happened in her past, she altered her emotion (anger). Together, her thoughts and emotions affected her actions (outcome). She essentially needed to make a quick second decision about how to change her focus, but she did not.

As you are reading, think about how YOU might begin to learn and apply this material. Also, think about when you might apply some of these ideas and actions into competing. Some athletes find certain skills work best for them as part of their overall warm-up, while others might find seek mindful practices for cool down or recovery, finding them best to use at the end of a training or competition. Find some way to practice these skills, just like you practice your sport, so that you can better use the tools when you need them most, within your practice or competition, and ultimately, within your life.

CHAPTER 2

MINDFULNESS: OVERVIEW

A Brief History of Mindfulness and Mental Tools

In the 1950s, psychologists focused on observable behavior. They primarily looked at what happened before a behavior (antecedents) and after a behavior (consequences) to understand actions and reactions. For example, if athletes had an anger management problem, that approach would target something in the environment, something that had provoked their behavior, or something which rewarded or reinforced the behavior in some manner. The treatment for the anger problem was to change the environmental factors triggering it.

Around the 1970s, a growing number of psychologists began to put forth the idea that in order to understand behavior it is important to consider the internal processes of the individual, not just outside influences, to understand behavior. For example, what is the athlete thinking? What are his beliefs about his performance? What is this person saying to himself? This became known as cognitive psychology. Cognitive anger management therapy might have looked at helping the athlete change his thoughts about the situation. The environment was not the only factor to consider; the internal self-talk and beliefs were also important in understanding behavior.

Later, the two approaches to understanding behavior were joined, and cognitive-behavioral theories and therapies developed. Psychologists began looking at both the environment and the athlete's thought process to fully understand behavior. Many sport psychology techniques have a foundation in this approach, such as imagery, goal setting, and self-talk skills. In fact, research has indicated that the more successful athletes had high self-confidence and used the psychological skills of imagery, positive self-talk, goal setting and maintaining concentration (Taylor, Gould & Rolo, 2008, Thomas, Murphey, & Hardy, 1999).

Today, there is a growing movement toward mindfulness as a practice and a tool in psychology (Davidson & McEwan, 2012) and in the sport psychology field (Zizzi & Anderson, 2017). A mindfulness-based approach is considered a current framework for helping athletes with using psychological skills for performance. The objective of this approach is to help competitors become more aware of their thoughts instead of trying to eliminate certain thoughts, which was often the goal in early cognitive psychology frameworks. Some athletes and coaches continue to teach this. The goal of this book, then, is to help athletes learn and understand mindfulness, and this idea of awareness, because it is the foundation of many other sport psychology tools. To repeat, the goal is to not get rid of thoughts but to be aware and make choices for the focus of one's attention.

What Is Mindfulness

Mindfulness is both a way of being and a tool one can use to build mental flexibility. In general, it is a process that promotes awareness. For the purpose of this book, mindfulness is not the same as meditation. We view these as different constructs. Meditation will be discussed as a tool to enhance mindfulness. So, what does mindfulness mean to athletes?

According to Jon Kabat-Zinn (2004), author of numerous mindfulness books, mindfulness is about paying attention in a particular way, on purpose, in the present moment. There is also a nonjudgmental quality to it. Mindfulness is about being in the present moment, which means not dwelling on past events, such as mistakes, or anticipating future events, such as winning or losing. In fact, when athletes describe being 'in the zone', they often describe a sense of being fully aware, present and having a sense of flow (Csikszentmihalyi, 2007).

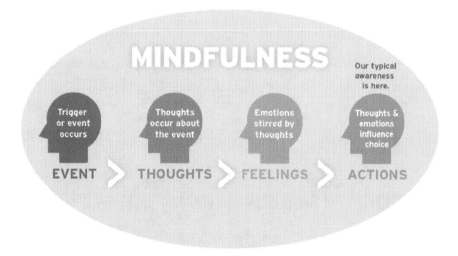

Overall, the idea is not to get rid of thoughts, or to have no thoughts, but rather to allow thoughts to occur without judgment. This is like watching cars on a highway. Cars can be symbolic of our thoughts and can race past us. We can either watch them drive along, or we can hop in the car. We can follow a thought and get pulled in a certain direction. The same idea was expressed by Thich Nhat Hanh in relation to emotions:

Feelings come and go like clouds in a windy sky. Conscious breathing is my anchor.

— Thich Nhat Hanh —

For example, Deb hopped *in a car. Her car took her down the road of blame and anger. This is very important to see because the action of jumping in the car of a certain thought happens so quickly. Mindfulness is the tool that can help Deb learn HOW to notice that she jumped in the wrong car.*

Deb:

- *Event: Competitor dropped pole in her runway.*
- *Thoughts: How could this person do this to me?*
- *Reaction: She glared at her.*
- *Feelings: Angry, irritated.*

- *Actions: Stayed focused on the pole dropping and the other person; did not change her focus.*

Deb's mind remained technically in the past and on a negative event. How can she get herself to a new approach with a different focus?

Deb lost the present moment, and it affected her performance. One way to think of this is that her body was running in present time, but her head was focused on an event in the past. Her body and mind were in different places. This athlete could have used mindfulness as a tool to help her mind be more present. The idea would be to have self-awareness, that she needed to change her focus to present time, and in this way, both her mind and her body would be in the moment. The best way would be to first recognize her thoughts. If not, she could note her feelings as another clue that she needed to change. She can feel she is not in a good place.

Rather than relying merely on 'hope' to experience present moment awareness and flow while training or competing, it is more helpful to empower yourself and learn methods to help move yourself on purpose. Consciously move your attention to be in the moment. Mindfulness is a tool that can help take you to that place.

Foundation of Mindfulness

In his book *Full Catastrophe Living*, Jon Kabat-Zinn (2004) outlined the foundation principles of mindfulness. Several of these principles are important for athletes of all levels in order to understand and build their mental game.

The first principle is non-judging.

We have constant streams of thoughts about experiences occurring in our lives. Many of us lose time and energy judging those experiences as good or bad. Kabat-Zinn points out how this creates a, "Yo-yo mind," or mental teeter-tottering. When judging an experience, a person may have an, "In your head argument," going back and forth about that experience—such as an athlete judging a performance as good or bad, or a conversation as positive or negative.

Deb's mistake was judging the actions of the OTHER athlete. But she also was upset with herself at the end of competition. She admitted to having a 'yo-yo mind', as she was upset with herself for putting her focus on her competitor. She knew this was not helpful. She also could not stop thinking about how rude the athlete was. She was having mental teeter tottering, and unfortunately, many coaches do not know how to assist athletes in these situations.

It is very normal for any athletes to 'yo-yo' when thinking about thinking. For example, athletes sometimes comment about having negative thoughts. Then, they get mad and judge themselves about having these negative thoughts. This is often how thinking about thinking gets rolling. Athletes are often told by coaches or others to be positive or to not think too much. The problem with this advice is that many athletes don't know WHERE to put their attention. That internal struggle results in wasted mental energy and a lack of awareness of the present moment, which contributes to a less-than -ideal performance. It is a vicious cycle.

A great example of this is taking a toy away from a child because it is unsafe, but not giving the child a different toy as a focus. In this scenario, many children start to cry or get mad. Many people know to give the child a different toy, so there is a new focus and hopefully, the child will stop crying.

So, the same idea applies to Deb. *If Deb had used her mindfulness tool, she would have noted and became aware that her focus was on the other athlete. If she had taken her focus off the other person, she would then have had to put* *it somewhere else on purpose; on something more productive for her. She could find a way to regroup and bring herself back to her own task of mentally and physically doing a new run-through to warm up for the pole vault competition.*

The idea is to have a plan for this. One example is below.

A, "Cleansing Tool," That Athletes Can Use to Change Focus

I often recommend to athletes that they establish some specific point in their practice or competing environment that they can use as their 'cleansing' spot. What do I mean by this? Deb could have a spot at the indoor or outdoor track that she designated her refocus spot. A cleansing tool is like an erasure on a white board. The purpose is to find a way to redirect thoughts. For example, Deb could choose a spot on the point/scoreboard, or a spot on the fence surrounding the track, or wherever she chooses. When in a negative mental place, and with an awareness that she needs to change her thinking, she can look at this spot, or point, and use it to re-center. She can designate this as her 'cleansing tool' spot. She will, on purpose, turn to her spot and take some breaths and use positive self-talk. She needs to plan for this ahead of time, so when she needs it, she knows what to do. This can help her get out of judging her thoughts and instead, make a deliberate choice to change her mental focus. This relates to the second important principle, acceptance.

The second important principle is acceptance.

Kabat-Zinn (1990) described this as seeing things as they are or exist now and knowing not to waste time thinking about events that have already occurred. A basketball player who misses an easy lay-up in a game may dwell on the missed shot. A runner or swimmer who doesn't like a lane assignment may stew over how the lane isn't the right one. In these instances, accepting the present moment or situation is a valuable skill that can help an athlete direct his or her focus. This sounds simple, but it takes a very strong mind to switch focus in an instant, especially when intense emotions, like anger or embarrassment, get activated.

Acceptance does not mean the athlete likes the situation. Instead, acceptance means not placing your focus on what you do not like or want and instead accepting these conditions and moving your mind, on purpose, giving yourself a different and more productive focus. This quick skill lays the foundation for redirecting thought processes and making the next choice in the moment.

It gives that athlete responsibility for his or her own focus. It is also a controllable action which will be discussed more in the, "Goals," chapter.

Deb can *accept the incident with the pole, but she does not have to like it. The sooner she can just state that it happened and get herself to refocus, the better for her. She can talk about the incident after the competition is done.*

Finally, the third important principle is patience.

Non-judgment and acceptance are valuable tools in building a strong mental game in sport, but developing these tools takes time, practice, and patience. Athletes like results. Athletes like to take action. Practicing mental tools, just like other skills, can take time. This means patience with yourself. Many athletes have, "one and done," mentality with these skills. This means they try it once, and if it did not seem to work, they abandon it. **Stay with it and practice it more!** Why? Patience helps YOU. If you learn patience while learning a skill, you give yourself time to be good at something. We get better with practice. Practice and patience go together. The goal is failure because this means an athlete gets to build stronger mental tools.

Mindfulness and Meditation

A common question athletes from all sports ask regularly is, how is mindfulness different than meditation?

My answer is that mindfulness is a skill, while meditation is like a practice you can use to build this skill. Both are important for athletes. What exactly does this mean?

Deb, the pole vaulter, would know she is not having good focus when she glares at the person who drops her pole. When she has this mindful awareness, she changes her focus, even if she must shift 20 times. The idea is she has awareness to shift. How does she build this muscle of shift? Some would say meditation is the training to help build this muscle.

There are many different types of meditation practices, and you may want to take a class or read books to find a practice that works well for you.

Meditation is one method for building a stronger mindfulness muscle. One example of a type of meditation practice athletes can consider is known as Western Vipsassana meditation. Vipsassana meditation is a practice that puts emphasis on mindfully breathing or putting your focus on breathing for a certain amount of time (a timed practice) (Anderson & Waterson, 2017). This means your focus is on your breath as it goes in and back out. When your mind wanders, your practice is to notice and bring your attention back to your breath.

Deb, the pole vaulter, needs to do this, and she has committed to practicing this type of meditation at home each day for at least 10 minutes.

Athletes are building meditation practices into their training, and this is one example of a type of meditation some are using to build their mental muscle. Many teams are now adding this type of meditation into their overall training practices to help athletes with focus and stress management. There are other types of similar techniques. One of these is using a mantra, or a one-word phrase, (as compared to a breath,) for holding focus.

Personal Reflections: Meditation and Mantras

While I was competing as a sprinter in college, I developed my own mental tools to help me with my starts for the indoor 55-meter dash. I used a meditative type tool to help me focus. While standing at the starting line, I would say over and over, "Gun," which meant to me to focus on the gun sound to GO! I didn't know it at the time, but I was using a basic mindfulness technique, a mantra, so my thoughts could be no other place—not on other sprinters, not on my time, and not on my judgment of my readiness. I wanted a single focus. This helped me stay in the present moment and not have anxiety about the finish. I was using a mantra, a form of meditation, and it helped me not to over-think or focus on anxious thoughts.

— Kristine M. Eiring, Ph.D.

Playing point guard on a college basketball team meant I needed to think through many situations at any given moment. One of my positive thinking tools developed accidentally my sophomore year while listening to the national anthem. I had a mantra rolling through my head, and I found myself counting the stars on the American flag while I was listening to the anthem. I repeated, "Hustle, defense, shoot," star after star. By the end of the song, I had run through all fifty stars, and a new mindful, positive thinking routine was born. I continued this through my entire college basketball career and still find myself doing this while watching games today.

— Colleen M. Hathaway, D.C.

Foundational Tool of Mindfulness

Mindfulness is the key to making the most of the basic sport psychology tools of positive thinking, self-talk, goal setting, imagery, and recovery.

Mindfulness is knowing what mental tools and skills to use to help bring you, the athlete, back to the present moment—the moment that is most important for performance.

Consider this analogy of three gears. The first gear is the situation or event. Gear two is the present moment. Gear three is your response. Many athletes overreact to a situation and get lost in the story in our head, and we skip gear two. In essence, we jump from one to three, often mindlessly, and we may or may not make our best choice. Gear two represents that moment, the micro pause, in which we make a choice for how to respond. Mindfulness and meditation trainings help us improve our use of gear two. In a nutshell, training the mind helps an athlete to lengthen the pause. With this skill, a different choice can be made which can affect better outcomes.

CHAPTER 3

MINDFULNESS = AWARENESS + ACCEPTANCE + ACTION

M any athletes confuse mindfulness with meditation and think the goal is to NOT have any thoughts or to completely eliminate negative thoughts. However, you will always have thoughts. The goal is not to stop thinking, but to have awareness, and flexibility, in your thinking. Through mindfulness, you will realize that you have many moments of choices and can decide on which thoughts you want to focus and which ones you do not. You have so much self-power in your mental focus so learn this. You are not at the whim of all your thoughts.

Have you ever noticed that you engage in a dialogue with yourself on just about every topic throughout the day? You have good thoughts, neutral thoughts, and critical thoughts. Thinking is a habit—something you do automatically. We tell ourselves incredible stories of events. A great example is the pole vaulter.

"You are only as strong as you are flexible in mind and body."

— Colleen Hathaway, D.C.—

For example, Deb *wondered in her mind if the person had dropped the pole on purpose. Then Deb talked to herself about how she would never do that to another vaulter. This story intensified when her coach came over and talked with her. He agreed she would never let that happen, and he also began getting mad, reinforcing some of the negative, angry thoughts Deb was telling herself.*

Has this ever happened to you?

Athletes think during training and while competing. Those thoughts can be helpful or not helpful, and we may not even know how our thoughts are influencing us from moment to moment. Many athletes hear from their coaches, "You need to think positive!" However, many athletes do not know how to move into different thinking or mindsets. They may just worry about not thinking the right way, and these worries make things worse.

Mindfulness is a skill that helps athletes gain awareness about their internal chatter. We often have numerous thoughts occurring very quickly. Some we follow, and some we do not. Mindfulness is about utilizing and giving more attention to those thoughts that are typically associated with better performance.

The exact number of thoughts per day that individuals have is disputed at present and even the definition of thought is unclear in the research. Various numbers exist about how many thoughts per minute, and per day, we **think**. Yet, there is some skepticism about how to actually measure this. It seems what is better documented by sport scientists is that when athletes worry and think about screwing up, they are more likely to actually make mistakes (Beilock, 2010). Additionally, people tend to choke under pressure because they worry. Choking is defined, in this instance, as performing more poorly than you can do. In other words, you have the ability to perform better than you are actually performing (Beilock, 2010). So, when we have worry thoughts about our performance, or we try to not have those worries, our performance may be negatively impacted. Worry creates tension in the body.

Thoughts: Think of Them Like a Traffic Light

A tool we can use as a good framework to understand our minds is the traffic light. These lights switch between red, yellow and green. Green thinking means that you are in the flow, that you are present (fully in the moment) in your workout or competition. Red thinking is dwelling on what's wrong, worrying about events in the future, or focusing on all the things you don't like. Use this tool to help you switch. It is easy to remember and a guide you can use to know which color zone your thinking is in.

Research is showing a mind-body connection, and it seems that the more stressful the thoughts we have, the more stress hormones we produce (Sternberg, 2000). This means that if you think negatively, your body experiences more tension, which may lead to a poor workout or competition. When you start thinking negatively, you are likely to begin to picture a less-than-ideal performance. You struggle inside, trying to eliminate the mental image. This creates resistance or tension in your mind and body. By thinking 'red' thoughts, you are basically holding yourself back and not using your mental tools in a helpful way. Remember, you can check in with your body and have awareness of your tension, just like you can check in with your mind. Your mind and body both tell you something. Learn to listen. They are your guideposts to making changes in your mindset or self-talk.

What happens when you tell someone to think about a pink elephant?

What happens when you tell someone to NOT think about a pink elephant?

When you tell someone to think of a pink elephant, or to not think of a pink elephant, the result is the same. Both think of the pink elephant! You must direct your mind. Awareness is the tool that can help you switch those red thoughts into something more directive or helpful. This is a big step in reaching your goals more easily. The key is mindfulness, or the awareness that in any given moment you can purposefully choose where to direct your focus and thoughts. The beauty of this is that our thoughts are something we personally manage or control.

When Deb was pole vaulting, she could have told herself where to direct her focus rather than tell herself to NOT think of the pole, or the person who dropped it. By telling herself to visualize her routine, she is directing her focus. This is more productive, even if she has to repeat this step multiple times.

Personal Reflections

I have a clear memory of 'red thinking' while I was competing in the indoor USA track meet in Madison Square Garden, New York. I had qualified to compete in the indoor 60-meter dash. The first thing I checked when I arrived was the heat in which I was running. When I saw all the big-time sprinters in my heat, I instantly said to myself, "I don't belong here." Guess what? I didn't make the semi-finals. I never switched my thinking. It stayed red, and I didn't know what to do to help myself. I quickly lost my confidence.

— Kristine M. Eiring, Ph.D.

I, too, have a clear memory of 'red thinking, while playing in the NCAA basketball tournament in Iowa. There was a minute-and-a-half left in a game that was tied. I remember being fouled and going to the free throw line, and my thoughts were, "I'm not the right person to be at the line. I hope I don't miss." I did miss. I didn't have the awareness to switch my thoughts quickly, and I stayed with red thoughts. My brain looked for ways to help me miss, because that was what I was telling it to do.

— Colleen M. Hathaway, D.C.

What would you think about if all you told yourself was, "I hope I don't miss?" What image would you see? Would you see yourself making the shot?

Pushing Negative Thoughts Away Is NOT the Answer

When negative thoughts pop up, many athletes immediately try to push the thoughts away or cover them up with 'green' or positive thinking. This may help, but sometimes the scales tip. The athlete may try too hard to be positive, resulting in an internal conflict. You may have an unwinnable in-your-head argument between your 'good guy' and your 'bad guy'. You might say to yourself, "I shouldn't think this, but I am thinking this!" Many athletes than become mad at themselves.

Why is this an unwinnable argument? Because you cannot lie to yourself. You cannot be disingenuously positive at a time when you don't like your performance or you know you aren't performing at your best. It's hard to believe positive thinking in that moment.

So what do you do?

**"If there weren't yellow lights,
there would be a lot of crashes."**

~ Kelly Hathaway, age 9

Think Yellow Thoughts

Recall for a moment the ideas presented earlier on yo-yo mind or teeter-totter thinking. This is when an athlete swings from positive to negative thoughts, or visa versa. Yet, there is a space between these two opposites. This is the YELLOW zone, or the PAUSE.

It might be helpful to think of **non-judgment thinking** as "yellow," like those yellow traffic lights. Yellow thoughts are neutral, such as counting steps or simply focusing on one task or action (e.g., breathing or pumping arms). Yellow thoughts, for sake of analogy, are non-judgmental thoughts. You might also think of yellow thoughts as gear two.

In their book, The Psychology of Enhancing Human Performance, authors Gardner and Moore (2007) focus on this very idea. They write that we must naturally check in with our inner self and engage in self-adjustment at times. Athletes become more stressed when they primarily focus on thoughts of perceived deficits or self-doubt. The performer who can tune in to self-adjustments and remain neutral (yellow thinking) before ultimately shifting back into mindfulness, or present moment thinking (green thinking) can be more resilient. Neutral might be a good place to be rather than self- critical or red thinking. **How Can You Apply Non-judgmental Thinking to Your Sport?**

The Three A's: The Mindfulness Model to Learn and Use

So far, we have used two analogies to think about mindfulness. One is the idea of having three gears, and the other is the stop light with the three colors of red, yellow and green. We can turn those examples into three steps you can use to help yourself use mindfulness skills. The mental steps you will go through are:

1. **AWARENESS**. Be aware of your thoughts (mindfulness)

2. **ACCEPTANCE**. Accept what is happening. Don't argue about it in your head (nonjudgement).

3. **ACTION**. Adjust your thinking or focus if needed.

Closer Look at The Three A's

The **first step** is being aware of what you are saying to yourself or the nature of your thinking. This is mindfulness. You can do this by just taking a deep breath and checking in with yourself. Imagine you are in a cloud, looking down on yourself and listening to your thoughts. What do you hear? If you are hearing more red thoughts, such as "I can't do this," or, "everything is horrible," then move on to step two.

If Deb, the pole vaulter, would periodically check in with herself, as some athletes do during competitions, she might have caught herself thinking RED. Athletes might want to consider this idea of doing mental check-ins throughout practice or during competitions. A great example is a hockey player checking-in mentally between shifts, same for basketball players who are taken out for a rest. Those are great moments to do awareness check-ins.

The **second step** is accepting that you are thinking red thoughts. Fighting with these thoughts is unproductive.

Acceptance does not mean you like how you are thinking or performing. But ***acceptance*** is a tool to get off the 'yo-yo' mind. You need to name or label that you are thinking red and direct your focus elsewhere. For example, I have heard many athletes say, "I know I should not be thinking negative. I get so mad at myself when I do this." In this example, first you have "red thoughts," and then you mad at yourself for having those thoughts. You are jumbling your mind with thoughts about thoughts.

Either use the negative thinking as a way to fire up your emotions, like anger, and change or motivate yourself into different action, or change your thinking to something like this: "I am thinking I can't do this," and, "I can change my focus."

"I am thinking I can't do this," is different from, "I can't do this."

This is a small WORD CHANGE but a very BIG difference. You cannot change all of your thinking patterns, but you can recognize a thought, and you can choose to follow it or not. You can alter ONE thought in a moment. You can do this, and you need to know this.

The way to shift these conditioned 'I can't . . .' thoughts is through a mindful and non-judgmental awareness, by training your mind through repetition of the mantra, "I am only thinking that I can't." Quickly, a realization will occur: You do not need to believe everything that you are thinking, and you can make adjustments and choices.

> **"We never talk about what we can't do. We talk about 'here's what we need to do, so let's go out and do it.'"**
>
> *~ Brad Stevens, Butler basketball coach, quote from Wisconsin State Journal 3/24/11*

Finally, the **third step** to mindfulness is action. It is important to recognize that you have a choice in changing your focus or thoughts. There are many quick and simple actions athletes can take to refocus and adjust. Examples include taking a deep inhale/exhale breath, telling yourself to adjust, or even tapping yourself on your leg or arm. One of the best actions you can take to change your cycle of thinking, if you have more time, is strong physical exertion, such as a quick burst of sprinting or one minute of pedaling hard on a stationary bike. This action helps produce testosterone, which stimulates the frontal lobe of the brain and paves the way for more clear thinking.

You can also ask yourself some good questions. "Is there something I can think that's more helpful?" or, "What can I think of that would be neutral and more directive (yellow)?" Your brain will want to help you answer that. It works like a search engine on your computer. Ask it a good question.

For example, one simple path to a yellow thought is accomplished by asking this question:

What's Important Now (W.I.N.)?

W.I.N. is a simple, yet powerful, acronym that comes from Lou Holtz, the famous Notre Dame coach. By asking this question, you can begin guiding yourself back to the present moment, or at least to a neutral place. If you are in the middle of a competition, and you are not liking your performance, then answer the question by saying things such as, "I can refocus. I am okay. I can do this. I can take it one step at a time." Keep it simple.

Through mindfulness, you can accept that you are thinking in a certain way but also know that you have the choice to follow a different thought. This realization and acceptance can take time, or it can happen quickly if you practice. I like the example of our thoughts being like clouds. Imagine laying on grass and looking at clouds. When we get stuck on one thought, it's like looking at one cloud. Yet, the truth is we can see many clouds, and we choose which one we look at the most.

This is a good time to remember the cleansing breath or spot that was discussed in chapter one with Deb, the pole vaulter.

Recall that Deb *could have a spot at the indoor or outdoor track that she designated her refocus spot. She has decided her action step when thinking in the RED zone is to take a moment to focus on a spot on the point/scoreboard, or a spot on the fence surrounding the track, or wherever she chooses. When in a negative mental place, and with an awareness that she needs to change her thinking, she looks at this spot or point and uses it to re-center. Her mental tool is to use this 'cleansing tool' spot. She will, on purpose, turn to her spot, take some breaths and use positive self-talk. This is awareness, acceptance and action!*

Personal Reflections

After my sprinting career in college, I started to do some road races. I also began to swim more. Both of these activities were a big mental switch for me because there was more time to think in training and competing. Sometimes when I was distracted and had awareness that I was telling myself, "I don't want to do this," or, "I'm not good at this," I would switch my thinking to neutral. I would begin to count steps between markers, look at shoe colors of other runners, or even add up house address numbers in my head. All of these neutral thoughts were, and still are, really helpful in getting me to a more mindful mental place, which helps me run or swim better. I see these as 'yellow' steps taking me into the 'green' zone.

— Kristine M. Eiring, Ph.D.

In my early thirties, I began participating in longer endurance events. I had a difficult time 'minding my mind'. I would say things like, "I don't like running. My knees hurt. This is boring. I want to be somewhere else. I miss my teammates!" I experienced a dramatic shift in my thinking shortly following a seminar in mindfulness. It was there that I learned about "watching" my mind and not believing everything my mind was saying. I began to pay attention to my thoughts and name them as just thoughts. I learned how to tune into my breathing and stay with the exercise I was choosing. I have since completed numerous endurance events that I would not have been able to do without mindfulness.

— Colleen M. Hathaway, D.C.

Thinking as It Relates to Our Inner and Outer Environments

When we discuss negative and positive thinking, be aware that this applies to analyzing both ourselves and our outer environments, such as playing conditions. For example, you might have feelings of nervousness while competing. You might notice this and begin to think about it and judge it: "Oh, no! If I'm nervous, I might play badly." You have attitudes and thoughts about your 'inner world' and physical sensations, and then you dialogue with yourself about this. At the same time, you might also have attitudes and self-talk about others around you. You might focus on your opponent and talk to yourself about how prepared he or she is looking during warm-ups.

You start to think about yourself and question if you look that ready. Both instances, of internal and external worlds, involve you going into your head and having a dialogue. Both instances involve judgment, and both can be addressed via the three A's: awareness, acceptance, and action.

Building Reminders into Your Mental Practice

We've been recycling since at least the 1970s, but only recently has it become a world priority. One of the reasons for the change is that we see so many reminders about it. Think about the garbage bins used for recycling, the television ads, the signs at work and school, and the movement to conserve. We have constant reminders to change our behavior, so we are getting much better at 'thinking green'. We are becoming more mindful of our choices regarding how we treat our earth and environment.

This same idea relates to sport psychology. If you are to become mentally strong, you need not only tools and techniques, you need reminders to help apply focused green thinking. Focus is a mental muscle, which means you strengthen it by learning to redirect your attention over and over again. Visual reminders, such as notecards, colored shoestrings or a dot on a hockey stick, build mental strength by giving you a focus and a very quick reminder to be mindful.

Research indicates that to learn and apply one must repeat and practice. If this sounds like your basic training, it is. The mind and body are connected through repetition. The more we see, the more we do, and the more efficient we become. Building reminders into your mental practice is like making a grocery list. You know what you need but sometimes forget. The same thing happens with mental skills. You understand the concepts, but you need to see them over and over to build a strong mental set. It is like doing weight repetitions to build muscles.

Some important points to remember about mental tools and using visual cues include the idea that if you want to learn and apply a new mental skill, it is helpful to practice and use visual cues to help you with this process. Some great examples include having note cards or sticky notes with your reminders for mental focus on them. Place them where you will see them throughout the day. You can also hang meaningful posters or quotes in your locker room, personal locker, car or on your bathroom mirror. Or, wear a colored shoestring or wristband that acts as a reminder for you to focus on the present moment. Every time you see this, your brain will make a connection to your desired outcome. Specifically, you could hang notes in your house that have the word breath on them, so you remember and train yourself to build more awareness to use breath as a focus and mental tool. One great tool to build mind and body awareness is to have a coach blow a whistle in practice, and have everyone pause and do a mental check in. Ask yourself in this moment if any adjustments need to be made and make them.

"To build mental strength, you need to have repetition."

— Kristine M. Eiring, Ph.D. —

Use this chart to list the helpful thoughts and actions that you want to remember:

Helpful positive thought:	Helpful action:
I can do this	Breathe.
I'm okay.	Count.
Focus.	Focus on a spot or shoe or shirt.
I believe in me	Look at something in your environment.

Other helpful positive thoughts:	Other helpful actions:
_____	_____
_____	_____
_____	_____
_____	

Post this information where you can see it on a daily basis. Apply these ideas in other areas of your life so you can practice and build your awareness muscle.

CHAPTER 4

MINDFULNESS: GOAL SETTING

"Setting goals is the first step into turning the invisible into the visible"

~Tony Robbins

I t seems that how one defines success might be closely aligned to the type of goals one sets or is driven to achieve. What do you want to achieve? What is your plan to reach your goal?

For example, athletes can set goals to improve their personal skills. These might include such things as skill or conditioning development (speed, strength). Another type of goal is to gain certain awards or accolades. These two goals are very different but often co-exist. According to some, it may be important to have both of these types of goals. (Eliot, 2005).

A third goal might be to develop character. Character goals are about developing yourself as a whole person and different aspects of your sport help you achieve this.

Goals and Surrounding Culture: What is Your Definition of Success?

Coaches, family members and others all help to create a culture surrounding athletes. These people can influence goals a lot. "The behavior of coaches, parents, peers, and teammates has a powerful effect on the athlete's understanding of what achievement means. These individuals create an environment around the athlete that's known as the motivational climate" (Harwood, 2005, p. 23).

What does this mean?

Those watching athletes practice and compete can applaud and help reinforce high effort, cooperation, and shared contributions. They can also respond with punishment or negative feedback for mistakes. Some might give special treatment to star players. Stop for a moment and think about what type of messages were communicated to you as a child about your performance. If you are a parent or coach of a youth, think about how you might reinforce certain behaviors with your responses to the performance of the young athlete. The reactions from others can contribute to the sport climate and may impact the types of goals an athlete develops and values.

A parent of an athlete can praise effort even if their child doesn't finish in first place. Other parents can express disappointment if their child does not win. These different types of responses can influence the types of goals a person sets, especially if seeking praise.

Another way to say this is that it seems our goals, or how we define success, can be task-driven or ego-driven (Harwood, 2005). Athletes who have task-oriented perspectives are more concerned with effort and believe abilities can be improved. Athletes with ego-oriented perspectives see ability as somewhat set, and they tend to compare themselves more to others. They want to show what they can do, sometimes even at the expense of effort (Harwood, 2005). There may be some benefit in the pursuit of beating an opponent, of working toward winning as a main goal.

However, for athletes wanting long-term success, the development of task- or achievement-oriented goals is important (Eliot, 2005). Carol Dweck, a researcher at UCLA, discusses the idea of mindset in her book, Mindset: How You Can Fulfil Your Potential (2012) and the importance of having a flexible mindset. This applies to goal setting in many ways and seems consistent with the task-oriented type goals. The idea of a flexible mindset is that we can grow and change rather than our skill level is set and cannot change.

To date, research seems to support many advantages of having task-oriented goals. An athlete who has this perspective may engage less often in judgment or negative thinking and may therefore be more mindful. The thrill of getting better on certain aspects of one's game or sport is important in motivation development and seeing improvement in skills can ultimately lead to the desired outcome goal, such as passing your competitor in a race or getting a personal best.

Ego type goals are more about win/lose. An example of this is a basketball player who had decided success, for her, means she must be the team leader in scoring for every game. This is an ego type goal or an outcome goal. If she is not the point leader, she believes that she is not successful. This goal overlooks other aspects of her basketball games, such as assists and good defense, and possibly contributing in other ways that helped. She might have a fantastic game if she looked at these as goals to help with her overall game. She might even help her team win. In fact, she might be a better team player with a different goal. However, if she does not see those types of goals as successful, she may be critical of herself. Why? Because goals also help direct our attention and focus. Sometimes athletes actually hurt their team with these types of goals because the individual goals outweigh a team goal.

Goals play an important part in successful performance because we usually rehearse goals in our working memory. Athletes rehearse goals both by talking to themselves about their goals (self-talk) and by picturing their goals (imagery) (Cormier and Nurious, 2008). Goals also help athletes build training plans because athletes want to take action steps to reach their desired outcome. In this way, goals help create the expectation of success as athletes design their workouts in order to meet the desired goals. In this way, task goals and outcome or ego goals can work in tandem.

Types of Goals

Outcome and Process Goals (Small goals) and Character Goals (Big Picture)

Athletes and coaches typically set training and competition goals. Training goals often involve working on, and achieving, certain set points, such as lifting a certain amount of weight, reaching a particular batting percentage, or hitting a certain number of fairways in a golf round. These types of goals are called **outcome goals**. Most athletes are aware of these types of goals and often have long-term and short-term outcome goals set for a season. They are typically quantifiable goals.

What are some of your outcome goals for either a practice or your sport this season?

1. _____
2. _____
3. _____

There are times when **process or task goals** may be just as important, or even more important. Process goals mean exactly what the name implies—picking one specific action to focus your attention and using that action as a guideline for improvement. Process goals are about how you're doing something, not about the final outcome. *They're especially helpful if you aren't performing at the level you want or if you continually feel disappointed with your outcome.* For example, a sprinter may want to attend to knee lift or arm drive, a basketball player may want to practice ball release, and golfers may want to focus hip or shoulder rotation and make changes accordingly. These types of goals can help performance as athletes make changes in technique to help have more positive outcome goals.

Overall, mindfulness is having awareness as to what types of goals you need to focus on—outcome or process. But setting process goals ultimately helps you achieve outcome goals and can help with confidence building as well. It is sometimes more helpful to think of **how** you will move through your performance rather than the **end** goal of the performance. This is easy to say! A golfer once said that he had a poor performance on hole three and took that performance with him the next six holes until he finally realized he needed to change his focus to the present moment and his next shot ....on hole 10.

What process goals can you set for yourself? You may have different process goals for each practice or even for a competition.

1. _____

2. _____

3. _____

What are Character Goals? Questions to Consider

What kind of leader or teammate do you desire to be, and what character traits would you display in the following example?

The Lettuce Story

It is lunch time in the high school cafeteria. You drop a piece of lettuce on the floor. What do you do? You have many options.

- You can look around and guess if anyone else saw this.
- If not, you might leave it on the floor and walk away.

- You might casually shove it toward someone else and make it look like he dropped the lettuce.
- You might think its garbage, and the people who clean the cafeteria can pick it up.
- You can pick it up and throw it out.

What would you do? What does this say about your character?

Now, imagine you are a teammate who saw the person drop the piece of lettuce on the floor. What do you do? There are multiple choices.

- You can tell your teammate.
- You can pick it up.
- You can let it sit on the floor.

What does this say about the character of your teammate? Who do you want on your team and why?

Dr. Jim Loehr has spoken about character and has studied character and performance. He reported that data suggests there is a huge link between character and performance, and like our muscles, character traits can be improved.

Bo Hanson, four-time Olympian, described two types of character goals: Personal and Performance.

It seems personal characteristics drive performance characteristics. Personal characteristics considered positive include respect, honesty and integrity. Positive performance characteristics include self-discipline, confidence and resilience.

Character goals are really important in building good team culture and positive personal leadership skills. Many business executives and athletes have similar characteristics. They are often self-driven and have a winning mindset. They are willing to learn from their mistakes and take feedback. These character aspects are needed on great teams. There are some interesting statistics for athletes and leadership. Ernst & Young surveyed 821 high-level executives and found that 90% of women sampled played sports. Among women currently holding a C-suite position, this proportion rose to 96%. In addition, 95% of Fortune 500 CEOs played college sports. In other words, positive character traits are important for building better teams and better future leaders.

Goals and Visual Cues

Mindfulness can be part of this goal-setting process. You need to remember and stay aware of your goals.

Brain research shows that if we see something frequently, like a daily reminder of a goal, we are more likely to remember it.

That means you need to have visual reminders of your goals, preferably reminders that you will see throughout the day. When you see a visual reminder, you can say to yourself, "I'm working on that." It's like a training workout that is posted electronically. If you forget your workout routine, you see the posted outline, and your brain reacts with, "Oh, yeah, now I remember."

Goal reminders can be very simple visual cues, such as a swatch of color or an image on a hockey stick or a softball bat. Some people even wear different colored shoestrings so that they can look down, see the colors, and be reminded of their goal. Goal reminders can also serve as reminders to be in the present moment, which is a good practice.

Choose a goal reminder that is visual, and see how it helps you. What will it be? Teams can have a motto and put this on the wall where everyone sees it. They can choose certain behaviors they want to see from each other and give weekly awards to teammates who best display them. We need these types of visuals and rewards to reinforce the traits and behaviors we want to build.

Personal Reflection

Part of the reason a coach outlines a workout is to give structure and goals for the practice. A specific outcome goal for sprinting was sometimes completing several practice 100-meter sprints, each in a certain time. Process goals included high knees and strong arms without a specified time. The focus was on form. Our coach also emphasized character. We cheered for every person on our team. Track can be a really individual sport, but I believe his emphasis on supporting every athlete on the team was his method of character building. I believe this is what helped us be such a successful team overall (we won all four Big 10 Outdoor Team Track Championships while I was there) .

— Kristine M. Eiring, Ph.D.

Goals are vital for success in any athletic event. I have come to appreciate the idea that outcome goals give me a specific thing to focus toward—a number goal. In contrast, process goals remind me to pay close attention to aspects of my body or technique during a training or competition and to adjust accordingly.

— Colleen M. Hathaway, D.C.

Whether you set outcome or process goals, make sure that they follow the ARMS guideline.

ARMS

- *A*ction oriented: Know what you are trying to accomplish in practice or competing.
- *R*ealistic: Set goals that you can attain but that make you reach slightly for your next level.
- *M*easurable: If your goal is truly measurable, someone else should be able to tell when you've met your goal.
- *S*equential: Just as you break down a play or a routine into parts, consider having smaller goals that build on one another and allow you to work toward a bigger goal.

<u>Suggestions for Coaches</u>

For building character goals:

- Talk with your team or athletes about the larger meaning of sport. Character can be tied to motivation.
- Ask them some good questions: What kind of person do you want to be? What makes a good teammate?
- Give your expectations: I want players who 'pick up the lettuce'. I want players who help others and pick up the lettuce for their teammates.
- Ask your players to come up with some ideas about what character means for them. List them and

display them. Check in on them. Focus on one of the ideas each practice. Challenge your athletes to carry it over into the other parts of their life. Ask them to share when they fell short and how they will do better next time. Vulnerability and honesty are part of building character. These are goals players remember for life!

- Reward character behaviors that are positive. Unexpected praise can help reinforce the actions you are wanting to increase. Notice them being good! Tell them.

CHAPTER 5

MINDFULNESS: IMAGERY

Imagery is an important tool in sports. Some refer to it as visualization or mental rehearsal, and the terms are often used interchangeably. Imagery is considered a broader term than visualization as it highlights the integration of other tools one might include to enhance imagery, such as self-talk or guided verbal cues, body sensations and emotions.

Why is imagery important? Consider this: scientific data released from the National Institute of Health confirms that the mind and body function as one. Researchers have found, via extensive animal and human studies, that stem cells migrate from the bone marrow into the brain and become new neurons (Holzel, et al., 2011). In essence, the growth of brain cells never stops. This means you can learn, change, and grow with each new thought or image you have during the day. These new cells give rise to new thoughts, and mindful images are critical to what you create. You are what you think!

A French pharmacist in the 1800s is credited for helping promote the idea of imagery. He proposed it as a method to aid relaxation and thought it was important to think positive and not dwell on illnesses. He believed the power of the imagination can exceed the will and that it is easier to imagine relaxation spreading throughout your body than to, "Will it," (Davis, Eshelman, & McKay, 2006).

For athletes, it is important to use imagery as part of their mental game. Mental imagery can be used for many different reasons in sport. It can be used to recall and review a best performance or see yourself being successful while doing a certain action. It can also be used to mentally rehearse or practice a new skill in your mind. Just as athletes might learn by watching film of other great athletes in their sport, an athlete can also use his or her own mind to imagine a positive performance.

"The best way to cope with mistakes is to learn from them and see yourself making changes. The worst way to cope with mistakes is to continually imagine them."

—Kristine Eiring, Ph.D. —

Some researchers have found that some parts of your brain are activated in the same way whether you are experiencing an event or simply visualizing it. This means that it is very important to mentally imagine what you want to have happen. For example, some divers mentally rehearse their dive twists and moves prior to actually doing them. Distance runners see themselves in a race, practicing tactical moves in their minds. Studies seem to show that successful athletes use imagery more extensively than less successful athletes (Vealey & Greenleaf 2006). An interesting study done by Gregg and Hall (2006) showed that for some golfers, as their handicap increased their use of visualization decreased. In other words, it seems those golfers performing better may be engaging in mental imagery more.

Remember, imagery can be used to:

- Recall past successes and help build confidence
- Rehearse a move, play, or overall game plan
- Remain focused and stay present by seeing plays develop and unfold
- Remind yourself of your goal by seeing it happen in your mind

Using this skill in the best way often requires mindfulness. One image can create an entire story and an incredible amount of self-talk. Do you want to rehearse what you did wrong? No! You may want to review what you did as a way to make corrections, but you do not want to go over and over and over what went wrong. Unfortunately, many athletes do this and don't know how to break the habit. They finish a competition and focus on their mistakes. If you do this, you may want to consider a different approach.

Deb, the pole vaulter, could have used imagery as part of her reset after the pole was dropped in front of her. She could have paused, regrouped and mentally rehearsed going over the bar prior to her jump. Even better, she could have combined a positive image, directive self-talk and her breath to bring her focus back to the moment - and her jump. She could have used these tools to refocus rather than stay upset with the other athlete. Anger is not bad, but she could have used it differently. She could have used it as energy for these tools.

Replaying mistakes is like self-punishment. Some athletes believe that if they make themselves feel bad enough, they can somehow make up for the mistake. Do you believe this?

Moving beyond a mistake and recovering mentally is more important than replaying the mistake in your mind.

Why? Because if you continue to dwell on mistakes or on outcomes that you don't want, your brain might help you follow those negative pathways. Instead, when you make a mistake, learn from it. Decide what you want and visualize that action or outcome. Your brain will then know what it is that you want to accomplish. Mindful imagery is a learned skill at which athletes can become better with practice, similar to practicing other aspects of their sport.

Knowing your brain is changing every day is another reason to make a change in your thinking. Feed your mind healthy thoughts to help build new pathways. Apply the three A's of mindfulness:

- Awareness of a poor performance
- Acceptance of the fact that this was not the best you could do (accepting has nothing to do whether you liked something or not. It just means get out of judging it and move to a reset).
- Action could mean creating a mental image of what you want to have happen so that you are in a better place to make it happen in the future.

Again, Deb? *When she finished her pole vault competition, she could have asked herself three questions: What went well mentally and physically? What did not? What corrections would I like to make? She could then mentally visualize the corrections. This would be a much better way to learn and recover, plus get ready for the next competition. She is helping herself create a plan and mentally rehearse for how she wants to perform next time.*

We all develop patterns, ways of doing things, which may be helpful or not. To change habits, we must have mindfulness. If not, we continue doing what we are doing, whether it is working for us or not. Ask yourself some questions before you practice imagery. Is there an aspect of my performance I want to mentally rehearse and see myself doing something successfully? Am I learning a new skill in practice and can I add mental imagery as part of my training? Remember to place yourself in the visualization rather than just seeing yourself doing something. Incorporate all of your senses: sight, smell, touch, sound, and taste.

Mindfully state what you want: "I want to......."

Creating Imagery Scripts

Most commonly, imagery is used in sport is to recall a best performance and compare it with a worst performance as a tool to help build a positive imagery script for future performances. You can easily begin to create your own script. Simply write or verbally record your answers to the questions below. Use the information to build your awareness about a best performance as a first step. Answer these questions:

1. What was one of your best performances? Mentally recall this performance. (It should be one that you might describe as occurring with ease.)
2. Involve all your senses: sights, sounds, and smells.
3. Ask yourself these questions: Where was I? Who else was there? What were the conditions? What was I wearing? How I did feel emotionally? Did I do

something helpful in a pre-competition warm-up, such as play music?

4. How did time pass? Fast or slow?

5. Was I thinking about anything in particular?

6. Where was my focus? Was it on the competitors or on myself? Was I looking at things in my environment, or was I more quiet and inside myself?

7. Finally, put it all together and relive the moment in your mind.

Now recall your worst performance and answer the same questions as above. Afterward, compare the two images and notice differences. Use this information as part of your learning, and make changes accordingly. Just remember to mentally rehearse the positive changes and not dwell on the worst performance!

ACTION STEPS

- Use the above information to build your script. Remember to state what you want to do rather than what you don't want. The way to be sure is to complete this sentence: "I want to_____."

- Have mental images that match your desired outcome.

- Do 5- to 10-minute daily mental reviews of this script.

- Remember that mindfulness is about awareness. You must ultimately choose where to put your focus.

CHAPTER 6

MINDFULNESS: MEDITATIONS

"**When we achieve the right focus, when we are properly mindful of what we're doing, awareness and action merge.**"

— James Loehr, Ed.D. —

I n the beginning of the book we described mindfulness and meditation being different concepts. They are linked because meditation practices are a way to build a mindfulness muscle. Many athletes who have not been part of a meditation practice might have some preconceived ideas of what meditation entails. In this chapter we will review meditation in general terms and then describe two specific types of meditation that you can try on your own.

Meditation

First, why should you care about meditation if you are an athlete?

Research in showing us that meditation is associated with changes in brain structure (Holzel, et al., 2011). Researchers at Massachusetts General Hospital, found that one area of the brain affected by meditation is the prefrontal cortex. This area of the brain is involved in executive functions such as planning, decision-making, judgment, comparison of ideas, and memories. This area of the brain also affects performance. Though this research is considered preliminary, there is a growing body of research addressing the relationship of meditation with positive gains, including, including brain changes.

There are many forms of meditation. Some are based on a way of living, such as meditations grounded in Buddhism or Zen practices, some have a religious or spiritual qualities associated with them, while others are more grounded in basic mindfulness training with a focus on breath.

Some basic misunderstandings about meditation practices include:

- There is one correct method
- I should NOT have any thoughts
- I can't sit still for very long; therefore, I am not a good at this
- I think even more, and this is wrong (likely to occur as you are building awareness).

Below are examples of different types of meditations. You may want to try several methods to determine if there is one you prefer for building mental focus and stronger attention.

Simple Breathing Meditation Example

Sit or lay down in a comfortable position. Take a few moments to get comfortable and begin to be aware of your breathing. As you breathe in, you may want to say, "I am breathing in," and as you breathe out say, "I am breathing out." Words with breath can help strengthen a more present moment focus. Thoughts will creep in. This is normal. The idea is to allow them to occur but to make NO judgements about the thoughts. Instead, note your thoughts. The moment of mindfulness is the recognition that your mind has wandered. Bring it back and put your focus on your breath again, naming your breathing, going in and out. You can simplify the naming to 'in' and 'out'. Begin this practice as a five-minute meditation and work towards 10 or more minutes. This is a powerful brain training exercise making you aware of your thoughts and ability to focus. You will have thoughts, but the primary goal is to return your attention to naming the breath. This is the beginning of mindfulness and learning to redirect your attention.

Body Scan Meditation Example

TIP: **record this meditation on your phone and listen to the recording as a guided, personalized meditation.**

Lie down and breathe in slowly and deeply through your nose. Feel your abdomen move out and up as your diaphragm contracts and draws air into your lungs. Your chest should not rise noticeably. Repeat this deep breath two times.

Now as you breathe in, direct your attention to your left foot. Feel your foot. Wiggle your toes and become aware of how your left foot feels.

As you breathe in through your nostrils, slowly scan your left leg from foot to knee. Feel the sensations in your lower leg. Simply become aware of them. Accept any tension or discomfort. Scan slowly, up through your thigh now.

As you breathe out, bring your awareness from your leg back down to your foot. Do this three times, with awareness of the sensations you feel in your left leg. If thoughts appear, then simply name them as 'thoughts'. Gently come back to your breath, and shift awareness over to your right foot.

Slowly inhale while and direct your attention to your right foot. Move through the same process you used with your left leg. Wiggle your toes in your right foot and become aware of how your right foot feels. As you breathe in and out, move your attention from your foot to your knee. Move your attention to your right thigh. Continue to note your thoughts without judgement. If your mind wanders, bring it back to your leg.

Exhale and scan back down s-l-o-w-l-y. Do this three times, with awareness of the sensations you feel in your right leg. Simply accept all sensations, name them, and feel what happens. Relax.

Now focus on your stomach. Feel it rising as you breathe in and sinking as you exhale. Your heart rate will begin to slow down. This is normal. Remain aware of your breath and your stomach as it moves up and down. Become aware of any sensations.

Now follow the same procedure with your left hand and arm as you did with your leg. You may clench your fist at first to really direct your awareness to your left hand. Breathe in and scan your arm beginning at your hand and moving upward toward your shoulder. Exhale and scan your arm slowly back down toward your hand. Do this three times.

Now scan up along the length of your right arm, to your shoulder, and then back down your arm to your hand. Breathe and scan your right arm three times.

Bring your awareness back up to your chest. Continue scanning up along your neck and to your face. Gently clench your jaws, and release as you exhale. Feel the sensations in your jaw and your throat. Breathe and scan. Feel how the back of your head rests against the floor. Scan your head.

Now detach from focusing on any body parts. Breathe. Perhaps you can note how you feel and how everything is connected, resting gently on the floor. Just breathe, letting any sensation come to you. Breath is nothing you have to chase after. It just is. Accept it as a part of you, and name it. Return to your breathing. Just breathe for a minute and feel your body. Then sit up slowly and end your body scan meditation.

ACTION STEPS

Use one of the meditation examples to practice daily. It may be your mind wanders a lot. That is okay. That is normal. The idea is to gently name your thought and return your focus to the task. This is similar to what you must do in a practice or a game. When your mind wanders, you bring it back. This helps build attention for the present moment. You can also choose your own meditation or possibly get one of the many apps for your phone so you can listen to a meditation easily.

**"The breath is the intersection
of the body and mind."**

—Thich Nhat Hanh —
Breath Meditation (St. Ruth, 1998)

CHAPTER 7

MINDFULNESS: BODY CONNECTION & RECOVERY

"You must be 100% committed to each action. If there are doubts in your mind, your muscles won't know what to do."

— Gary Mack from his book Mind Gym —

Mindfulness and Recovery

Have you ever followed a link to a song, article or movie? This process allows you to take information from one source and transfer it to another source, such as your phone. Think of recovering from an athletic event as 'downloading' important information you want to store and transfer to your next event.

Why is recovery important?

Among athletes, recovery isn't talked about very much. Competition and practices end. Athletes shower and eat and move on with life without taking the time to mindfully recover. However, there might be many things still happening in our bodies and minds that relate to our event or training.

For example, when we are finally quiet, usually at bedtime, sometimes thoughts about our performance and things that did not go well creep into our minds. That activates a tension pattern in our brain and muscles. Then, at the next event, we might recall the 'bad' things (and hope they don't happen again) and tension forms in our body. We may become anxious and wonder, "What if the things that went wrong last time happen again?" These thoughts and physical reactions to memories happen quickly. This is why recovering with mindfulness is vital to athletic success. Mindfully concluding a practice or competition means noting what when well, what did not, and what we might change next time. In this way, we are more consciously placing our attention where we want it. We might make a mental goal to do something different next time. We take time to know what we want to work on in our next practice so we are ready to compete at our best.

Creating a Mindful Recovery

Creating a mindful recovery plan can be very helpful. Consider the suggestions below and create your own mindful recovery plan.

1. First, consider getting into a restorative pose (see image): Following your event, allow your heart rate to return to a normal rhythm, and then make your way into restorative pose. Sit directly next to a wall and lay on your back while raising your feet up the wall. Place a pillow or blanket under your hips if that's more comfortable for you. Position your legs as close to the wall as possible, allowing the heels of your feet to rest against the wall. Note: If you suffer from back pain or strain, check with your trainer or doctor before trying this pose or alter it so it is safe for you.

2. Next, take a deep breath by inhaling through your nose to a slow count of five. Then exhale out your mouth to a slow count of seven. Repeat this breathing exercise three times and proceed to Step 3 while remaining in restorative pose. (You can adjust the breathing count from five and seven to what you need.)

3. Apply the **three A's** while in restorative pose: **awareness, acceptance,** and **action.**

   • Awareness and acceptance begin with deep breathing.
   • Ask yourself three questions during your recovery:
     o What went well?
     o What did not go well?
     o What will I need to do better next time?

ACTION STEPS

Spend approximately 10 minutes in restorative pose. When you rise, immediately write your answers to the three questions. Do this after every training session and competition. The more you repeat this process, the more mindful you can grow your attention muscle. You may also look for any patterns that emerge in your answers.

Additionally, you might consider adding this step to your recovery practice. Take the three things you wrote that you did well and write each one on a green sticky note. Post the notes in places where you will see them throughout the week, such as on the bathroom mirror or car dashboard, or in a locker or desk. This is a great way to help you recall positive aspects of your training and mentally rehearse seeing them.

One of the goals of this exercise is to have more attention on what went well, or what you can correct, instead of what went wrong or other types of thoughts that can add to tension. You want to be mindful of knowing when to switch your thinking—and how. Recovery time is a good practice to build awareness and for using mindfulness tools.

If you drive a car with the parking brake engaged, the efficiency of the car is decreased. The engine works well, but the output is slowed. The same is true for how our thoughts affect our body. Fearful thoughts slow us down and can create tension in the body. Many fearful thoughts begin with 'what if' statements:

- What if Coach didn't like my performance?
- What if this happens again in the future?
- What if I keep missing my shot?
- What if my serve is bad next time?

'What if' thoughts are associated with anxiety, muscle tension, and a decreased ability to think quickly in a situation. To work through 'what if' thoughts, end your practice or training with mindfulness, and use recovery to help you improve your athletic performance. Review the chart below for ways to replace anxious or 'mind-less' thoughts with mindful thoughts.

Remember: A relaxed mind = a relaxed body.

Mindful-less Thoughts	Mindful Thoughts
I can't...	I am strong.
What if I fail?	I have a relaxed focus on....
I always perform badly at this location.	I am breathing.
I am never going to...	I see my green reminder, which means go!

Here is space for you to write your own thoughts based on your sport:

Mindful-less Thoughts	Mindful Thoughts

CHAPTER 8

MINDFULNESS: FINAL THOUGHTS

"When your heart is in the game, you have passion. When you have passion, your heart is in the game. Either way, you will most easily have mindfulness with heart and passion."

—Kristine Eiring, Ph.D.—

After reading this book, you have the tools you need to begin training your brain to be fully in the moment. Mindfulness is an ongoing process. You will get better at it with practice and time, but be patient with yourself as you go.

One day soon, you'll find yourself applying the principles of mindfulness without having to remind yourself to do so. You'll experience flow, fully enjoying the present moment, and when you do, you'll most likely find yourself performing more successfully, too. The best performances occur when you are present—not regretting the past or worrying about the future or the outcome of the event.

Mindfulness is a fantastic tool you have as an athlete, and it can take you to new places in training and competition. Mindfulness can also reignite your passion and your sense of fun. When you become less critical and judgmental and work more on solutions, you might gain more energy and motivation to keep improving.

Think back to when you first experienced the sports you compete in today. Were you a child? A teenager? Did you go into the sport dreaming of great success, or did you pick up the sport because you thought it was fun?

Chances are, you were drawn to a sport because you enjoyed it. Yet, as we advance in a sport and become more serious competitors, we often lose that sense of fun—of pure passion.

Through mindfulness, you can find your way back. When you're not judging your performance, when you're focusing on the sheer movement of your body and the skills you're developing, you're experiencing the sport as you once did, with glimpses of the way you did as a child. You begin to remember what you enjoyed about the sport.

So be in the present. Reignite your passion. Practice mindfulness, and see where it will take you!

Thoughts from Kris...

Gratitude

I have searched for meaning as to why I like to be so active and have decided that engaging in sport is a form of expression for me. There is a physical expression in movement, and words do not fully capture this expression. When competing, I have had moments of feeling connected to something far greater than myself. I have also had moments of being really low and exhausted, which lead me to search even deeper sometimes. All of these moments have helped me in my overall life. I am learning there is no ONE destination in life. There is a continuous process with each day giving me an opportunity to be slightly better than yesterday. This is the same for sport. There is no spot of perfection. Each day you work to get a little better at your craft. One constant for me has been the choice, that no matter the weather or life circumstances, I can tie my shoes strings and go for a run. This clears my head. I breathe deeper. I discover new trails or see a city differently as I run the sidewalks. I can be among people but very much inside myself. It's quiet here. I find solace in moving.

I am grateful to so many people who have inspired me with their books and wisdom. Coaching Evelyn, Dan Millman's book, *The Peaceful Warrior*, were early reads for me that helped me connect spirituality with sport. Others that have impacted me include Jon Kabat Zinn, *Wherever You Go There You Are, North to the Night*, Carlos Castaneda who wrote *The Teaching of Don Juan*.

Thank you to so many of the athletes I have worked with in sport psychology. You inspire me with the way you work through challenges and handle pressure. The highs and lows of sport have made many of you great human beings. I am lucky to have had the opportunity to work with so many high caliber people. For all this, I am grateful.

Services

The authors of this book are happy to work with teams to apply these concepts. We are available to do team or coach trainings that meet your needs. Please contact them for more information.

APPENDIX

Remember, **the first step to change is awareness**. Use these worksheets to help you develop awareness in your sport.

Using Imaging/Visualization to Build Your Awareness

1. Do you use mental imagery to prepare for a new technique/play or a competition?

2. If yes, do you place yourself in the visualization or simply observe it?

3. What helps you to create your own positive images?

4. Do you create imagery of what you WANT (vs. Not Want)?

5. Do you imagine how you want to feel during your practice or competition?

6. Do you involve all your senses?

Awareness of Your Best Performance

1. Where was your focus right before you competed? Did you have a routine you followed?

2. Where was your focus during your competition?

3. What kept you connected to the present moment?

4. What did time feel like? Did it pass quickly or slowly?

5. Did you use any mental tools that helped you succeed?

6. Describe the sensation of 'flow' or of being 'in the zone'.

Mindfulness and Confidence Building

1. Do you set task goals for yourself each practice?

2. What are words and mantras you can use to help you build your confidence?

3. Do you know what to say to yourself to help yourself recover from a mistake?

4. Are you able to receive compliments? If no, how will you change this?

5. Do you use recovery tools to help you recall your gains, growths, and successes?

Mindfulness, Sport and Practice

1. Have you created a daily mental program for yourself?

2. What techniques do you use to practice your mental game? Examples might include keeping a journal and writing your goals and mantras on a daily basis, using note cards to remind you to focus, using a meditation to practice, etc.

3. Do you include some mental imagery as part of your warm-up for a practice or game?

4. How will you use mindfulness tools to help yourself with a recovery after practice or a performance?

REFERENCES

Anderson, M. & Waterson, A. K. (2017). A brief impressionistic history of paying attention: The roots of mindfulness. In S. J. Zizzieand M. B Anderson (Eds.). *Being Mindful in sport and exercise psychology: Pathways for practitioners and students.* (pp. 17-30). Morgantown, WV: FIT

Beilock, S. (2010). Choke. New York: Free Press

Cormier, S. & Nurius, P. (2008). Interviewing and change strategies for helpers. Pacific Grove, CA: Brooks/ Cole-Thomson.

Csikszentmihalyi, M. (2007). Finding flow: The psychology of engagement with everyday life. New York: Basic Books.

Davidson, R. J. & McEwen, B. S. (2012). Social influences on neuroplasticity: Stress and interventions to promote well-being. *Nature Neuroscience*, 15, 689-695. doi: 10.1038/nn.3083.

Davis, M., Eshelman, E. R. & McKay, M. (2006). The relaxation and stress reduction workbook. Oakland, CA: New Harbinger Publications.

Dweck, C. (2012). Mindset: How you can fulfil our potential. London, UK: Robinson

Eliot, J. (2005). Motivation: The need to achieve. In Shane Murphy (Ed.), The sport psych handbook. (pp. 3-18). Champaign, IL: Human Kinetics.

Gardner, F. L., & Moore, Z. E. (2007). The psychology of enhancing human performance: The mindfulness-acceptance-commitment (MAC) approach. New York: Springer Publishing Company.

Gregg, M. & Hall, C. (2006). The relationship of skill level and age to the use of imagery by golfers. *Journal of Applied Sport Psychology*, 18(4), 363-375.

Harwood, C. (2005). Goals: more than just the score. In Shane Murphy (Ed.), The sport psych handbook. (pp. 19-36). Champaign, Il: Human Kinetics.

Holzel, B.K., Carmody, C., Vangel, M., Congleton, C., Yerramsetti, S. M., Gard, T., & Lazar, S. (2011). Mindfulness practice leads to increases in regional brain gray matter density. *Psychiatry Research: Neuroimaging*, 191(1): 36 DOI: 10.1016/j.pscychresns.2010.08.006

Kabat-Zinn, J. (2004). Full catastrophe living. London, England: Piatkus.

Loehr, J. (1982). Mental toughness training for sports. Lexington, MA: The Stephen Greene Press.

Mack, G. (2001). Mind gym. An athlete's guide to excellence. New York, NY: McGraw-Hill.

Mezey, E., Chandross K. J., Harta, G.,Maki, R. A. & McKercher, S. R. (2000). Turning blood into brain: Cells bearing neuronal antigens generated in vivo from bone marrow. Science, 2001 Apr20: 292, 438-440.

Rooks, J. D., Morrison, A. B., Rogers, S. L., & Jha, A. P. (2017). "We are talking about practice": The influence of mindfulness vs. relaxation training on athletes' attention and well being over high demand intervals. *Journal of Cognitive Enhancement*, 1-13. Doi: 10:1007/ s41465-017-0016-5.

Sternberg, E. (2000). The balance within: The science connecting health and emotions.

W.H. Freeman and Company, New York, NY.

St. Ruth, D. (1998). Sitting: A guide to Buddhist meditation. New York, NY: Penguin Group.

Taylor, M. K., Gould, D. & Rolo, C. (2008). Performance strategies of U.S. Olympians in practice and competition. *High Ability Studies*, 19, 15-32.

Thomas, P. R., Murphey, S. M., & Hardy, L. (1999). Test of performance strategies: Development and preliminary validation of a comprehensive measure of athletes's psychological skills. *Journal of Sports Sciences*, 17, 697-711.

Vealey, R. & Greenleaf, C. (2006). Seeing is believing: Understanding and using imagery

in sport. In Jean M. Williams (Ed.), Applied sport psychology. (pp. 306-343). New York: NY: McGraw-Hill.

Zizzi, S., & Anderson, M. (2017). (Eds). Being mindful in sport and exercise psychology: Pathways for practitioners and students.

Morgantown, WV: FIT

Printed in the United States
By Bookmasters